in Tudor times when the two towns were formed into a single boro
replaced the rope-ferry that then plied between the two sides of the

In 1789 George III arrived in Weymouth to spend a holiday by t
had been born. Wealthy visitors promenaded on sands that until rec
rubbish dump, or braved the waters in the then new pastime of 'sea
have been Weymouth's glory days, but the arrival of the railway confirmed its reputation as the
perfect place for a 'bucket and spade' holiday by the
sea.

Today, the beaches are as popular as ever, and the
Harbour waterfront, with its shops, restaurants and
pubs, remains full of character. Inevitably, the town
has expanded, but villages such as Bincombe and
Upwey, nestling in the lee of the rolling downland
that forms Weymouth's backdrop, retain much
of their charm.

By contrast, Portland is much

more dramatic. Its geology is extraordinary, but the Portland you see now is more than the product of great natural forces that took place 145 million years ago, for few places have been so completely transformed by man. Every age has left its mark. The raids made by the Vikings were the first on the English mainland. By 1066 and the Norman Conquest it was already a royal manor, an honour it retains to this day.

Across the top of the Island medieval farmers laid out long strip fields, some of which survive – despite the ravages of quarrying. For Portland is best known for its stone, so much of which has been removed that it is sometimes jokingly said that there is more of Portland off it than still on it. From its quarries came the stone for Sir Christopher Wren's masterpiece, St Paul's Cathedral, and the Cenotaph memorial in Whitehall.

Until recently, development was dominated by the Royal Navy, who as sail gave way to steam transformed Portland into the home of the Channel Fleet, complete with breakwaters and massive defences. The Navy has now gone, allowing tourism and the sea to play an increasingly important role. For Portland is best enjoyed in the open air. Few places pack so wide a variety of landscapes into so small an area. Its coves, cliffs, old quarry cuttings, and surviving farmland continue to evoke a lovely pastoral atmosphere, enhanced by the summer song of the skylark.

Weymouth from the air. In the foreground
are the Nothe Gardens, whose steep slopes
provide a natural shelter for the Harbour. On the right is
the Nothe Fort, built in Victorian times, and now open to visitors. Beyond the Condor hydrofoil
ferries that make the short sea-crossing to the Channel Island lie the famous sands and the Esplanade.

Weymouth Harbour, with the picturesque houses lining Nothe Parade and the
wooded slopes of the Nothe Gardens on the right. The Harbour is still used commercially, and
fishing remains a vital industry.

ABOVE The Harbour Master's office, cafés and pubs line the historic Custom House Quay. This is one of the most popular parts of town, full of bustle, day and night.

RIGHT Heading seawards for a night sail. The twin leaves of the Town Bridge are raised several times a day for boats entering or leaving Weymouth Marina.

BELOW Weymouth Marina. Dredging and pontoons have turned the Backwater into one of the most sheltered marinas on the south coast, whilst the waterfront is now home to apartments, a cinema and shopping centre.

Weymouth's Georgian splendours so dominate its architecture that it is easy to ignore its other buildings.

ABOVE The 400-year-old building in Trinity Street was Weymouth's first 'Assembly Rooms', to which a new wing was added in the 1700s for balls and concerts.

BELOW The artist Sir James Thornhill (1676 – 1734) was born in what is now the White Hart public house. Amongst Thornhill's masterpieces is the painting inside the great dome of St Paul's Cathedral.

ABOVE St Mary's Church was designed by celebrated local architect James Hamilton, and was completed in 1817. Close by in St Mary Street once stood an ancient friary. St Mary's was built in the Regency period of elegant simplicity. The smooth exterior walls are of fine-jointed Portland Stone ashlar. Above the triangular pediment on the west front, a single bell hangs under a pillared dome.

LEFT The grid pattern of the streets of Old Melcombe Regis, at the heart of what is now Weymouth's town centre, dates from medieval times. Many historic buildings line the charmingly narrow St Alban Street.

OPPOSITE PAGE Floral decorations on the Georgian bow-windows of Brunswick Terrace enhance the sunny seafront setting.

ABOVE The separate sea front terraces merge into a continuous backdrop when seen from the beach at low tide.

OPPOSITE PAGE A great boost to Weymouth's popularity came with the arrival of the railway in 1857. This colourful little train of a different sort takes modern tourists along the Esplanade. Behind are the twin pinnacles of the Royal Hotel, which opened as Weymouth's first hotel in 1772 and boasted a Long Room in 'which one hundred couples could dance with ease'. The present building dates to 1897.

BELOW The weathervane in Greenhill Gardens is a replica of the Supermarine aeroplane, a predecessor of the Spitfire, and is a memorial to Weymouth aviator George Stainforth who established a new world speed record of 406.92 mph in the 1931 Schneider Trophy Contest.

Between 1789 and 1805 George III and the royal family spent 14 summers in Weymouth. In honour of their royal patron, its citizens commissioned a large statue of the king, resplendent in his robes and guarded by a magnificent golden lion and white unicorn, to stand on a Portland stone plinth at the start of the Esplanade.

grateful Inhabitants
GEORGE THE THIRD
On His entering the 50th Year
Of His REIGN.

J. HAMILTON.
ARCH.

ABOVE The chalk figure of George III on his favourite grey horse on the hillside between Sutton Poyntz and Osmington was cut in 1808, three years after the king's final visit. The original sketch was drawn by James Hamilton, the architect who designed St Mary's church and the most elegant of the Georgian terraces.

RIGHT The ornately decorated Jubilee clock has long been a focal point on the Esplanade. It was erected in 1888 to mark Queen Victoria's Golden Jubilee. Until recently it was where the townspeople traditionally gathered to see in the New Year.

BELOW The bronze statue of Queen Victoria, facing her predecessor George III at the other end of the Esplanade, was unveiled by her youngest daughter, Princess Beatrice in 1902.

Sun, sea and ice-cream – and buckets and spades and
Punch and Judy on the sands.

ABOVE The annual Weymouth Beach Kite Festival attracts champion flyers from around the world. Some of the weird and wonderful kites are up to 30 metres long!

RIGHT Tutankhamen, complete with Egyptian temple and pyramids, appropriately all of sand. Weymouth sand sculptor, Mark Anderson, like his celebrated predecessors, creates his masterpieces using nothing but sand, water and colour.

High summer on Weymouth beach.

Weymouth is fortunate in having two nature reserves. ABOVE Radipole Lake is within a stone's throw of the town centre. Over 250 species of birds have been recorded, and the reserve is managed by the Royal Society for the Protection of Birds. On the right is the thatched Information Centre.

BELOW The reserve at Lodmoor is also managed by the RSPB, and is a true flood plain fed by the water from the surrounding hills. Lodmoor Country Park is also the home of the Sea Life Park, a sanctuary for the preservation and study of marine species, including seals and sharks.

ABOVE The villages surrounding Weymouth are still largely rural, with much to enjoy. The Upwey Valley, here seen from Windsbatch Hill, is one of the most picturesque parts of Dorset.

BELOW The River Wey enters the sea via Radipole Lake, but begins as a series of springs, of which the best known is the Wishing Well at Upwey, where in Victorian times a two-arched recess was built into the hillside alongside the spring head.

BELOW The River Wey is still a tiny stream where it adjoins Church Street. Yet its mill race is sufficient to power the Upwey Water Mill, which despite being over 200 years old has recently had a turbine installed and is now generating hydro-electric power.

LEFT Nottington Spa House is one of Weymouth's most unusual buildings. For centuries a natural sulphurous spring here was believed to have medicinal healing powers, bringing travellers to sip or wash in its waters. In 1830 it was developed as a spa and for a short period was one of Dorset's most popular attractions – even though the smell of the waters was 'like the scouring of guns' and its taste that of 'a very hard boiled egg'.

BELOW At Broadwey the River Wey divides; one channel passing through a mill race, the other briefly becoming a ford. Between Upwey and Broadwey the river passes some of the most beautiful small country houses in Dorset, each of them in their own landscaped parkland.

Until the 1920s the lower Wey Valley was open to tidal sea water, and is probably the site of a Roman port where supplies for Dorchester were landed. Nearby lie a trio of historic buildings, all built of Portland stone; Radipole Old Manor, the 800-year-old Church of St Ann, and the former village schoolhouse.

The church's unusual triple bell turret is just visible to the left of the Old Manor. The Old Manor was remodelled in 1580, and until the Dissolution of the Monasteries belonged to Cerne Abbey.

The tiny farming hamlet of Bincombe is easily overlooked when driving along the main road between Dorchester and Weymouth. Reached along a lane, and sheltered by the Ridgeway, it is the quietest and most secluded of all the settlements around Weymouth.

ABOVE Rolling chalk downland surrounds the tree-covered village of Sutton Poyntz.

BELOW The village pond at Sutton Poyntz. Nearby is a Victorian water pumping station which itself is of such interest that it has its own little museum.

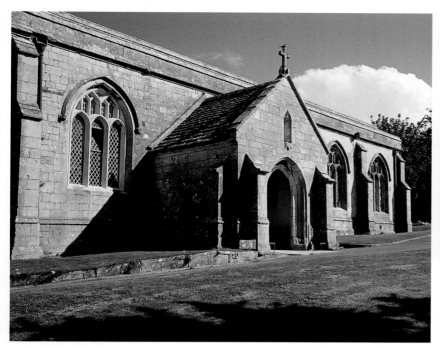

ABOVE One way of approaching Portland is along the Rodwell Trial, a pleasant 2¼ mile-long footpath and cycle track following the line of the old railway between Weymouth and Ferry Bridge.

ABOVE All Saint's Church, Wyke Regis, was once Weymouth's parish church, and the interior has changed so little that entering through the porch is like stepping back into the 15th century.

BELOW The historic stronghold of Sandsfoot Castle was built in Tudor times as one of a chain of coastal defences for Henry VIII. Together with its partner, Portland Castle, on the opposite shore, it was intended to protect shipping anchoring off Portland. You can reach it through ornamental gardens from Old Castle Road.

ABOVE The ruins of Sandsfoot Castle are still prominent on Weymouth's southern shore, which features several sheltered coves along the Portland Harbour frontage.

BELOW Almost the entire length of the Island of Portland is visible in this photograph of its west coast. Footpaths from Wyke Regis provide lovely views and glorious walking, not just of Portland, but of the Fleet lagoon and Chesil Beach.

The Island and Royal Manor of Portland from the air. The pattern of medieval strip fields can clearly be seen, now much diminished by development and by the quarries of the world-famous Portland Stone. The lighthouse with its red strip round the centre is clearly visible on the extreme southern tip of Portland Bill in the foreground, whilst in the background are Portland Port and the Harbour breakwaters.

ABOVE The land sheltered by Chesil Beach was once a tidal inlet called The Mere. Once reclaimed, it was dominated by enormous fuel storage tanks for naval ships and Europe's biggest military helicopter base – HMS Osprey. Both Navy and helicopters have gone, and the area is now a maritime leisure and business complex known as Osprey Quay. In the foreground are Portland Marina and the Weymouth and Portland National Sailing Academy.

BELOW Looking out over Chiswell and Underhill towards Osprey Quay. On the left are the Fleet lagoon and Chesil Beach, a unique arc of pebbles which extends for 18 miles to West Bay. Although Portland is an island only in name, it was virtually cut off from the mainland until the building of the first bridge at Ferry Bridge.

RIGHT A racing catamaran gathering speed off the Weymouth and Portland National Sailing Academy, the host venue for the 2012 Olympic and Paralympic Sailing.

The centre was opened by HRH Princess Anne, the Princess Royal, in 2005. At this same place a decade earlier her brother Prince Andrew, Duke of York, commanded the largest flying unit in the Fleet Air Arm.

LEFT Portland Castle is one of the best preserved of Henry VIII's coastal forts and is a popular visitor attraction. Like Sandsfoot Castle (see page 21) it was intended to defend Portland Harbour. Even today, the symbolic keys of Portland's three castles are presented to the authorities for safe-keeping at the annual 'Ceremony of the Key's' at Portland Castle.

A harbour within a harbour. The sun sets over the 600-berth Portland Marina.

ABOVE A strong sea wall in Chesil Cove protects Chiswell in this vulnerable corner of Portland's coast. The promenade is a good place to enjoy the delightful view across Lyme Bay, and to experience the bracing sea air.

BELOW Cyclists pause on West Cliff. The massive rock structures were built in the early 19th century to support a rail tramway for tipping quarry waste over the cliff.

Old cottages in Mallams. Historically this was a separate hamlet, but it is now part of the Underhill 'metropolis'.

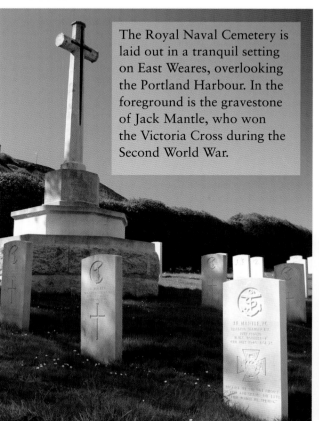

The Royal Naval Cemetery is laid out in a tranquil setting on East Weares, overlooking the Portland Harbour. In the foreground is the gravestone of Jack Mantle, who won the Victoria Cross during the Second World War.

ABOVE The Victorians transformed the vast anchorage known as 'Portland Roads' into one of Europe's greatest harbours by building four breakwater arms, a Herculean task that took civilian contractors and convicts 50 years to complete. The Royal Navy left the harbour in 1995, and it is now a commercial port. The panorama is best seen from the lookout near the north entrance to the Verne Citadel.

BELOW The Officers Field – a former sports ground – has been developed as the Olympic Village for the 2012 sailing events, before being sold as private housing.

ABOVE AND LEFT 'The Spirit of Portland' by local sculptor Joanna Szuwalska, is a stunning representation in Portland Stone of a stonemason and a fisherman. It was erected on common land below Portland Heights at the dawn of the new millennium. The position commands a sweeping panoramic view over Chesil Beach and the mainland coast.

BELOW In the 19th century virtually the entire summit of Verne Hill was remoulded for the construction of the Verne Citadel, one of a series of massive fortresses on the east side of Portland built to defend the Harbour and its approaches. As well as the ramparts earthworks, and ditches in the two photographs below, much of the work is hidden – tunnels, sallyports, dungeons and casements. The Citadel is now HM Prison The Verne, a training establishment for prisoners.

St George's Church at the top of
Reforne is one of Dorset's finest
Georgian buildings. It was designed
by a local master builder, Thomas
Gilbert, whose grandfather had been
Christopher Wren's quarry agent at
the time of the building of St Paul's
Cathedral. Most remarkable are the
matching pulpit and reading desk and
the hundreds of exquisitely carved
headstones in the churchyard.

ABOVE Easton Gardens – at the heart of Tophill - is an oasis of trees, and colour, surrounded by a bustling square. They were opened in 1904 amid a blaze of Edwardian optimism. Easton Methodist Church (left) of 1907 displays some of the best examples of the stone carvers' art on the Island.

BELOW Countless centuries of habitation, through hardship and prosperity, have given historic Wakeham a rich heritage of buildings. Simple stone cottages mingle with taller Victorian houses; some perhaps built with stones first quarried and squared in medieval or even Roman times. This street is full of character.

ABOVE AND BELOW LEFT The little thatched treasure trove of Portland Museum was established in two old cottages at the bottom of Wakeham in 1932, through the efforts of Dr Marie Stopes, the birth control pioneer. It is a lovely and rare survivor of Portland's 16th and 17th century architecture, and is a superb place to embark on the discovery of Portland's remarkable history.

RIGHT Pennsylvania Castle was built in 1800 as a 'marine mansion' for John Penn, Portland's Governor, and grandson of the founder of Pennsylvania, USA. It stands on one of Portland's most attractive sites, overlooking Church Ope Cove, and enjoys sweeping views of the English Channel.

OPPOSITE PAGE For Portland's first church, the Saxons levelled a platform, sheltered among trees in a steep bank high above Church Ope Cove. It was demolished in the 12th century and only a few fragments have been found.

The church of St Andrew that replaced it, in the same position at the foot of the dell below Rufus Castle, was of exceptional quality, reflecting the wealth and importance of the Royal Manor. We know from excavations that it was quite elaborate; its windows were glazed with a transparent mother-of-pearl tint, which must have shed a most beautiful light onto the Purbeck marble shafts and paving inside.

The form of the old church can be clearly made out from the remnants of ancient walls and pillars. It is now a truly romantic ruin in a sylvan setting.

ABOVE One of Portland's oldest and best-loved ancient monuments (right) overlooks the beautiful Church Ope Cove. The medieval Rufus Castle was vital for the defence of the Island, but its early story remains largely a mystery.

BELOW Ancient tombs in the graveyard of the ruined St Andrew's Church.

RIGHT In the past, Church Ope Cove was the scene of well-documented smuggling activity. Here too were ancient stone-shipping piers. The beach, once used extensively by local fishermen, is overlooked by popular recreational huts.

BELOW Solid reminders of Portland's flourishing agrarian past, a pair of stone windmill towers still dominate the skyline between Weston and Wakeham. Their long-lost sails last turned in the 1890s, and many of the fields that fed them are no more.

OPPOSITE PAGE BOTTOM This part of the east coast of Portland was the scene of the second largest landslide ever recorded in the UK. Some of the vertical cliff faces became obscured by rock falls and tipped overburden from centuries of quarrying, but verdant nature has now covered the slopes. Many grassy footpaths meander around the botanically rich Weares below, and the round-the-Island walk along the clifftop is now part of England's long distance South West Coast Path.

Visible out to sea is the notorious Race off the Bill, which can reach 7 knots at spring tides and cause dangerous overfalls and heavy breaking seas.

Considering its size, Portland's churches are some of the most interesting in Dorset.

ABOVE LEFT All Saint's Church, Easton Square, is the Island's parish church. In 1984 hundreds of colourful kneelers were made to mark the 70th anniversary of its founding in 1914.

ABOVE RIGHT St Peter's Church was built by the convicts working on the Breakwaters in the 19th century, and is a supreme example of their ability to work and cut stone to the highest of standards. It was designed by a captain in the Royal Engineers as a garrison church for the soldiers stationed at the Verne Citadel and was completed in 1872. The mosaic flooring in the porch and sanctuary was made by women prisoners at Parkhurst.

BELOW Avalanche Church (St Andrew's), Southwell, was built to commemorate one of the most tragic of Portland's shipwrecks – the collision between the clipper *Avalanche* bound for New Zealand and the sailing ship *Forest* in 1877. The bubbles in the stained glass windows, made by local artist Jon Callan, and which seem to rise from depths of dark blue to the translucent surface of the sea, represent each of the 106 lives lost.

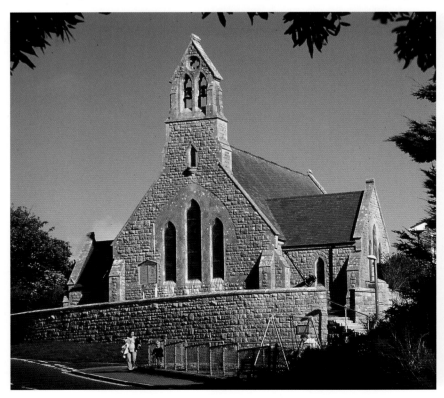

ABOVE At Longstone Ope, near the Bill, the Coastal Path passes long-abandoned old coastal quarries, and rare remnants of the traditional hand cranes.

RIGHT The world renowned Portland Stone has been cut and carved into some of the nation's best-loved buildings. The skills of traditional quarrying have now given way to mass excavation and high-precision mechanisation. Just a few years ago, these houses at Avalanche Road looked across ancient fields; a pastoral patchwork bounded by timeless drystone walls.

LEFT Many old quarries, once teeming with industrious quarrymen, are now major recreational areas. Tout (the ancient name for a look-out) behind West Cliff, has become a nature and sculpture park.

ABOVE Looking north from the top of Portland Lighthouse towards the Old Lower Light, now an important bird observatory and field study centre. The area is well-known for its holiday huts. The old coastguard cottages are on the left.

LEFT For nearly two centuries Portland Bill had a pair of lighthouses – the Higher and Lower Lights – working in tandem, the first being built in 1716.

Following a terrible storm in 1901 in which several ships were lost in the Channel it was decided to build a new lighthouse on a site close to the Bill. It was lit for the first time in 1906, automated in 1996, and its powerful beam is visible 18 miles out to sea on a clear night.

RIGHT The Old Lower Light, seen here under a full moon, is often floodlit to attract moths and other nocturnal creatures for study. The beam from the 'new' lighthouse, beyond, gives reassuring guidance past this treacherous part of the Channel.

Spectacular storm waves rise over a great underwater ledge, creating the
notorious Portland Race. The stone obelisk was erected in 1844, long
before the the building of the lighthouse, to mark the extremity of the land.